Basics Of The Faith

Emily Zondlak

Chapbook Press

Schuler Books
2660 28th Street SE
Grand Rapids, MI 49512
(616) 942-7330
www.schulerbooks.com

Basics of the Faith

ISBN 13: 978195716989

eBook ISBN: 978195716996

Library of Congress Control Number: 2024922716

Printed in the United States.

Have you ever tested yourself to see if you are in the faith? In this book I explain the nine principles that are fundamental to believers in Jesus Christ. I want to lay a solid foundation in Jesus Christ, in which God has blessed me with His knowledge, understanding, and wisdom through our intimate time together through the years.

Before I explain the nine fundamental principles of faith in Jesus Christ, it's extremely important to believe and know that you have salvation in Jesus Christ. Salvation can mean a person or a place. It's an escape and brings comfort when the world seems to be falling apart. Salvation in God means that He sent His Son Jesus Christ to earth to be your deliverer. Father, Jesus Christ, and Holy Spirit are all references to the same Godhead or 3 Persons in One. Jesus is the deliverance from guilt and sin that you commit by the choices that you make in life. When you understand right from wrong is when you can have salvation in God. When you understand that you deserve nothing, yet Jesus died for you; this is when salvation begins. In the Book of Acts chapter 4 verse 12 says, "Salvation is found in no one else, for there is no other name under heaven given to mankind by which we must be saved." It's through Jesus Christ that all people can be saved. Jesus is the Way to God and enter eternal life, in which states in the Gospel of John chapter 14 verse 6. You will be persecuted for your faith and love for Jesus in this life, but stand firm in Christ because one day very soon, your eyes will see the Lord's glory!

What does being saved mean? In life, there's a constant struggle or battle of you behaving in such a way that one, you act how you want to, or two, you try to and live according to what is pleasing to Lord God Almighty, the Maker of the Heavens and earth. In Romans chapter 10 verse 9 states, "If you declare with your mouth, "Jesus is Lord," and believe in your heart that God raised him from the dead, you will be saved." When you are of age to understand right from wrong, you can be saved and make the decision to be born again. It does not matter if you are five-years-old or 195; just believe without having the slightest doubt in your heart, confess with your lips that Jesus is Lord and you shall be saved!

In the Gospel of John chapter 3 verse 16 Jesus says, "For God so loved the world that he gave his one and only Son, that whoever believes in him shall not perish but have eternal life." You need to believe in your heart and confess with your mouth the Name of Jesus. When you do and make this life-long journey decision, you and Holy Spirit are co-partners in life. Daily reading the Word of God (Bible) and praying (having conversations with God) are keys to understanding Him, believing in Him, and trusting Him.

All the evil that you have done is called sin. With a new attitude in living for Jesus, your mind and desires will change. You must turn away from known sins; repent to God and ask for forgiveness of sins. When you acknowledge that God is your deliverer, God is faithful and just to forgive your sins! He doesn't and won't remember your sins if you sincerely ask for forgiveness! In 1st John chapter 1 verse 9 says, "If we confess our sins, he is faithful and just and will forgive us our sins and purify us from all unrighteousness." Unrighteousness means that your wrongdoing God forgives anything and everything that is not in conformity or agrees with His will and purpose. In Psalm 103 verse 12 David says, "As far as the east is from the west, so far has he, God removed our transgressions from us." In the Book of Hebrews chapter 8 verse 12, Jesus says, "For I will forgive their wickedness and will remember their sins no more."

There are nine principles that are fundamental for believers in Jesus Christ to mature into faith and love. To give you a desire to live a godly life that is pleasing to God. The nine principles are based out of the Book of Hebrews chapter 6 verses 1 and 2.

Repentance means that you are conscious of the wrongs that you have done and you are willing to ask God to forgive you. It can mean a change of mind, which brings regret or even remorse on account of sin or wrongs, but not necessarily a change of heart. Repentance is a true sense of your guilt and turning from it to God; walking with God in the way of His commandments. When you realize that you need God to have compassion and mercy on you, this is true repentance. In your vulnerability, you should realize that what God has always seen you to be and declares you to be is your true identity. You then realize God is orchestrating this change in your heart.

In life, there are moments that everything is going well, you are seeking and serving God with all your heart, and you have joy. Mountain top experiences! But wait, you find yourself traveling through the valleys, in which life seems to be falling apart. In these valley moments, you aren't seeking or serving God with all of your heart like you once did. The first fundamental principle of sound doctrine is repentance from acts that lead to death and a few examples of it are found in Revelation (the last book of God's Word,) starting at chapter 3 verses 1 through 3, Jesus says, "To the angel of the church in Sardis write: These are the words of him who holds the seven spirits of God and the seven stars. I know your deeds; you have a reputation of being alive, but you are dead. Wake up! Strengthen what remains and is about to die, for I have found your deeds unfinished in the sight of my God. Remember, therefore, what you have received and heard; hold it fast, and repent. But if you do not wake up, I will come like a thief, and you will not know at what time I will come to you." What Jesus is saying is that although you say that you are a believer because you speak the believer's language, you are dead inside. You started off seeking God wholeheartedly by reading, studying His Word, as well as having daily communication with Him. Nothing could damage your quality time with God! But hardships and life events happen that tug on your heart. These may start you to question your faith in God. You aren't eager to spend your quality time with God or to help by lending a helping hand to others for various reasons. Your faith in God was strong and powerful in the beginning, but then life happened and you decided to quit serving God. Jesus wants you to stand firm and strong in your faith; not becoming weary in the storms of life! As you grow spirituality, the storms of life become opportunities to see God work!

In Revelation chapter 2 verses 2 through 5 Jesus says, "I know your deeds, your hard work and your perseverance. I know that you cannot tolerate wicked people, that you have tested those who claim to be apostles but are not, and have found them false. You have persevered and have endured hardships for my name, and have not grown weary. Yet I hold this against you: You have forsaken the love you had at first. Consider how far you have fallen! Repent and do the things you did at first. If you do not repent, I will come to you and remove your lampstand from its place." In the beginning toward the middle stage of your intimacy with God, you didn't want to disobey God or hang around with people who completed wicked schemes. You knew when you persevered and endured hardships for Jesus that the trials were maturing you for the next phase of your faith journey with God. Since these stages have past, you aren't excited to spend quality time with God like you once did. You may choose to not share God's gospel as well as His promises and truths with others; when otherwise you would share. God desires you to repent, turn to Him, and to fall in love with Him all over again; spending quality time with Him as well as serving wholeheartedly! If you don't repent, God will pay you by what your actions deserve. Yet God will give you grace. Grace can be defined as God's favor, kindness, and friendship. God knows everything about you; every thought to every mistake. God gives His mercy, which means that God shows you compassion and forgiveness when it is within His power to punish. Grace is a gift to you that you don't deserve. God blesses you with grace to fulfill His calling on your life.

In Revelation chapter 3 verses 15 through 19 Jesus says, "I know your deeds, that you are neither cold nor hot. I wish you were either one or the other! So, because you are lukewarm—neither hot nor cold—I am about to spit you out of my mouth. You say, 'I am rich; I have acquired wealth and do not need a thing.' But you do not realize that you are wretched, pitiful, poor, blind and naked. I counsel you to buy from me gold refined in the fire, so you can become rich; and white clothes to wear, so you can cover your shameful nakedness; and salve to put on your eyes, so you can see. Those whom I love I rebuke and discipline. So be earnest and repent." As a wholeheartedly or displaying a passionate intimacy with God believer, you may not be practicing God's promises or truths that God has in His Word in your daily life. You may not know how to fight the good fight of faith well. You attend church, but you don't actively pursue God to know Him or to be known by Him. God desires you to seek Him by actively pursuing Him when reading and studying His Word, praying or talking to Him about whatever that's on your heart, and communicating with fellow believers about life's triumphs and tragedies for encouragement. You should be all in with God; not having one foot in God's kingdom and the other foot in the world; going with the flow in whatever the world says. God wants your entire being to be surrendered to Him; following Him in every season every step of the journey! When you trust and obey God, He blesses you abundantly; more than you could ever think or imagine! So be eager and enthused to pursue God intimately because He loves you immensely! Ask God to renew your faith.

All sins and wrongdoings can be forgiven if you sincerely repent. But there is one sin that cannot be forgiven, which is blasphemy against the Spirit. Blasphemy is the act of insulting or the lack of reverence to God and His divine being. Jesus says starting in the Gospel of Matthew chapter 12 verses 30 through 32, "Whoever is not with me is against me, and whoever does not gather with me scatters. And so I tell you, any sin and blasphemy can be forgiven. But blasphemy against the Spirit will not be forgiven." In the Gospel of Mark chapter 3 verses 28 and 29 Jesus says, "Truly I tell you, people can be forgiven all their sins and every slander they utter, but whoever blasphemes against the Holy Spirit will never be forgiven; they are guilty of an eternal sin." Blasphemy against the Holy Spirit means that you knowingly deny the power and authority of the Holy Spirit. But if you are scared and worried about blaspheming against the Holy Spirit, you haven't because you are conscious about not blaspheming.

The repentance from acts that lead to death principle means that you have remorse or deep regret about your guilt and sins that you have committed. True repentance is when you are walking away from your sins and turning to God because you know that your life with Him is a better life than a life without Him!

You, believer in Jesus Christ can rely on the Apostles' Creed which is a summary of the most important aspects and the basics of faith in God. Here is the Apostles' Creed:
I believe in God, the Father Almighty,
    Creator of heaven and earth,
in Jesus Christ, His only Son, our Lord,
    who was conceived by the Holy Spirit,
    born of the Virgin Mary.
    He suffered under Pontius Pilate,
    was crucified, died, and was buried;
    he descended to hell.
    On the third day he rose again from the dead;
    He ascended to heaven,
    and is seated at the right hand of God the Father Almighty.
    From there he will come to judge the living and the dead.
I believe in the Holy Spirit,

the holy Catholic Church,

the communion of saints,

the forgiveness of sins,

the resurrection of the body,

and the life everlasting. Amen.

Faith in God or faith towards God is the next principle in the sound doctrine depending on which version of the Bible, God's Word, you prefer using. I use the New International Version (NIV) so in Hebrews chapter 6 verses 1 and 2 uses the words faith in God. There are instances when I refer to the Amplified Bible and the English Standard Version Study Bible of God's Word to explain things thoroughly. Most Scripture verses are from the New International Version, but when I use the other versions, I reference which version I'm using. During my study, the Holy Spirit led and guided me in using the Apostles' Creed as a framework as I learned what the principle of faith in God meant.

Faith is the matter of your heart and how much or how little you are willing to have faith in God. Your heart can be described in four ways, in which the Parable of the Sower explains them in Matthew chapter 13 verses 18 through 23. Jesus says, "Listen then to what the parable of the sower means: When anyone hears the message about the kingdom and does not understand it, the evil one comes and snatches away what was sown in their heart. This is the seed sown along the path. The seed falling on rocky ground refers to someone who hears the word and at once receives it with joy. But since they have no root, they last only a short time. When trouble or persecution comes because of the word, they quickly fall away. The seed falling among the thorns refers to someone who hears the word, but the worries of this life and the deceitfulness of wealth choke the word, making it unfruitful. But the seed falling on good soil refers to someone who hears the word and understands it. This is the one who produces a crop, yielding a hundred, sixty or thirty times what was sown."

What is faith? For some of you, faith means that seatbelts or chairs can hold you. Also, you can say that you have faith in gravity and oxygen because you know that it's there. In other instances, faith can be described as believing in God and Jesus Christ is God's Son. Some of you think that faith needs to make everything fall in to place easily for it to be God. For the others, you don't have faith because too many people as well as other things have disappointed or hurt you. In Hebrews chapter 11 verse 1 as well as verse 6 describe what faith is. "Now faith is confidence in what we hope for and assurance about what we do not see. And without faith it is impossible to please God, because anyone who comes to him must believe that he exists and that he rewards those who earnestly seek him." God is 3 Persons in One. God the Father is the One who plans out everything that is good! Jesus Christ is Father God's Son and He has power as well as authority over everything because Father God has given it to Him. God blessed Jesus as being a carpenter Son. God is Jesus' Father, but on earth Jesus' parents were Joseph and Mary. Joseph's occupation was in carpentry so Jesus learned this skill too. How I imagine God completing His will and plan is God speaking to Jesus while Jesus is sitting on God's right-hand side of the throne. Jesus is writing down notes while God is speaking. Jesus comes up with the blueprint and lays out how God's plan is going to work so that the Holy Spirit can carry out God's plan and purpose on earth. Holy Spirit is the power source in the Deity in the Godhead. The Deity agrees with one another so He can't go off and do His own business that He may want to do. The Godhead has always been here since the beginning of creation of the earth. In Genesis chapter 1 shows the Godhead when everything started. Genesis chapter 1 verses 1 and 2 say," In the beginning God created the heavens and the earth. Now the earth was formless and empty, darkness was over the surface of the deep, and the Spirit of God was hovering over the waters." When you read Genesis chapter 1 further, it mentions how God spoke everything in existence. In Genesis chapter 2 verse 4, you can see the person switches from God to Lord God. Lord God refers to Jesus Christ so you can insert Jesus Christ's Name in the spaces that refer to Lord God. Genesis chapter 2 verses 3 and 4 say, "Then God blessed the seventh day and made it holy, because on it he rested from all the work of creating that he had done. This is the account of the heavens and the earth when they were created, when the LORD God made the earth and the heavens." As I have explained God the Father, Jesus the Son, the Holy Spirit have always been here; before the beginning of time.

Before I explain Jesus Christ was conceived by the Holy Spirit and born of the virgin Mary aspects of the Apostles' Creed, there will be recurring faith foundation phrases that I used to explain the nine principles of sound doctrine accurately. Some of you may think that I am being redundant and yet others may enjoy the redundancy because you understand that it helps you to remember.

If a man and a woman decide to get married, they have the choice to have sex to make love with each other. God may bless this man and woman with a baby as well as other children in the future. It's not a man's decision to make a woman pregnant. If a God fearing, God honoring, married man and woman kept themselves pure as well as holy (not having sex before marriage, keeping the marriage bed holy and sacred) God may bless this couple with children. But this didn't happen for Joseph and Mary when God chose them to be Jesus' earthly parents. God chose Mary because she feared or highly respected Him; honoring and following Him with her life! In the Gospel of Luke chapter 1 verses 26 through 35, Luke describes Jesus' birth. He says, "In the sixth month of Elizabeth's pregnancy, God sent the angel Gabriel to Nazareth, a town in Galilee, to a virgin pledged to be married to a man named Joseph, a descendant of David. The virgin's name was Mary. The angel went to her and said, "Greetings, you who are highly favored! The Lord is with you." Mary was greatly troubled at his words and wondered what kind of greeting this might be. But the angel said to her, "Do not be afraid, Mary; you have found favor with God. You will conceive and give birth to a son, and you are to call him Jesus. He will be great and will be called the Son of the Most High. The Lord God will give him the throne of his father David, and he will reign over Jacob's descendants forever; his kingdom will never end." "How will this be," Mary asked the angel, "since I am a virgin?" The angel answered, "The Holy Spirit will come on you, and the power of the Most High will overshadow you. So the holy one to be born will be called the Son of God."

Jesus lived a holy and godly life while He was in human form doing what God wanted Him to do. In Hebrews chapter 10 verse 9 Jesus says, "Here I am, I have come to do your will." Again, Jesus says in the gospel of Matthew chapter 26 verse 39, "Going a little farther, he fell with his face to the ground and prayed, "My Father, if it is possible, may this cup be taken from me. Yet not as I will, but as you will." Jesus was saying that the use of His body was the real fulfillment of God's will in regards to eternal life, the resurrection, and His holy Church.

Jesus' resurrection is powerful! Before Jesus was crucified on the cross, He had a Last Supper, in which He told His disciples that one of them was going to betray Him. Before Jesus was crucified, He prayed earnestly; wept bitterly that His sweat was like blood falling on the ground. Jesus was betrayed by one of His disciples with a kiss. This disciple handed Him over to be arrested because the world did not and continues to not believe in Jesus Christ or God the Father. Jesus' disciples abandoned Him and denied knowing Him. Jesus stood before the guards and they mocked Him. The guards made a crown of thorns and put it on Jesus' head, which pierced His skull. Jesus' garments were torn off from Him and were sold. The guards beat Jesus with chained whips that tore His body - it has been said that after Jesus was beaten no one recognized Him. That is how brutally Jesus was beaten! Jesus was questioned and falsely accused. The time came when Jesus was crucified on the cross and because of how brutally Jesus was beaten, Simon, a local person helped Jesus carry the cross to Golgotha. The guards whipped them along the way. At Golgotha, the guards stripped off Jesus' linen garments. With harsh treatment, nails pierced Jesus' hands and feet because He was hanged on the cross. Jesus was mocked again and insults were hurled at Him. Darkness plunged the earth. Luke chapter 23 verses 45 and 46 say, "And the curtain of the temple was torn in two. Jesus called out with a loud voice, "Father, into your hands I commit my spirit." When he had said this, he breathed his last." Jesus went down to Hades and conquered death because He rose from the grave and is seated at the right-hand-side of God!

Jesus was defeating Satan and death when His body was laid in the tomb for two days. On the third day, Jesus was raised to life! Jesus paid the ultimate price to save and release you from death. Jesus saved you from death and Satan's authority in your life. Satan's goal is to separate you from God, but Jesus defeated him and took away his power. For nothing, in all creation will be able to separate you from the love of God that is in Christ Jesus your Lord.

One day very soon, Jesus is coming to earth when God tells Him that it is the day and the hour! When Jesus along with His holy angels comes to earth, you who have passed away will be resurrected from the dead or raised to life again. You, believers in Jesus Christ, who are still standing strong living by faith on the earth, will not go before other believers who have passed away and are in their graves. Believers in Jesus Christ will rise first to be with the Lord forever. Jesus' resurrection is essential because you, as believers, can have intimate relationships with God, your sins are forgiven, and passing away or death isn't frightening if you believe in Jesus. You can have confidence in knowing that you will participate in the resurrection of the dead if you know that your name is written in the Lamb's Book of Life!

If you know, you need Jesus Christ to be your personal Lord and Savior, ask Him to come into your heart by repentance and confession because without faith in God your life is hopeless. If you believe in your heart and confess with your lips that Jesus is Lord, you shall be saved and will receive eternal life. According to the English Standard Version Study Bible, eternal life means a life of abundant joy and immeasurable blessing in the presence of God forever! When you believe in Jesus by deciding to make Him your personal Lord and Savior of your life, you will experience blessings from God, but not to the full capacity on earth as in Heaven. In the New Heaven and the New Earth you will experience the full measure of God's abundant blessings. Also, eternal life is the final reward and glory into which you, the child of God enter your Sabbath rest. Eternal life is beyond understanding, the endless life of the future, the happy future of the saints in Heaven. God is a gentle, merciful, and loving Father. He won't force you to be in an intimate relationship with Him if you don't want to. God blesses you with free choice; freedom to choose how to live your life. Your choice to accept Jesus or reject Him determines where you will spend eternity. It's either, Heaven with God, or in the Lake of Fire being tormented and separated from God, Jesus, Holy Spirit.

Jesus' Name is powerful. Jesus made a way for all of humanity to be saved and made right with God. Literally, Jesus Himself is living and dwelling in the inside of you. He gives you His power and authority to share His gospel with others, comfort those who are hurting, to free those who Satan has bound in darkness and slavery, and to help them see that only Jesus can completely satisfy them! In the Gospel of Mark chapter 16 verses

17 and 18 Jesus explains the signs that you as believers can do when believing in Him. "And these signs will accompany those who believe: In my name they will drive out demons; they will speak in new tongues; they will pick up snakes with their hands; and when they drink deadly poison, it will not hurt them at all; they will place their hands on sick people, and they will get well."

You are in the last paragraph of the Apostles' Creed. Remember I'm explaining the faith in God sound doctrine principle. The saints' communion is when you are fellowshipping or communicating with God as well as fellow believers. Communion is usually celebrated in a church; yet it doesn't need to be. Believers consume bread and wine, which symbolizes Jesus Christ's body and blood shed on the cross because of His great love for you, His child. Communion is a remembrance of the Last Supper, in which Jesus told His disciples that one of them was going to betray Him because He was going to be crucified on the cross. In Paul's 1st letter to the Corinthians chapter 11 verses 23 through 29 Paul says, "For I received from the Lord what I also passed on to you: The Lord Jesus, on the night he was betrayed, took bread, and when he had given thanks, he broke it and said, "This is my body, which is for you; do this in remembrance of me." In the same way, after supper he took the cup, saying, "This cup is the new covenant in my blood; do this, whenever you drink it, in remembrance of me." For whenever you eat this bread and drink this cup, you proclaim the Lord's death until he comes. So then, whoever eats the bread or drinks the cup of the Lord in an unworthy manner will be guilty of sinning against the body and blood of the Lord. Everyone ought to examine themselves before they eat of the bread and drink from the cup. For those who eat and drink without discerning the body of Christ eat and drink judgment on themselves." Examining your heart and your life is a way for you to repent from known sins and to choose to forgive anyone who has hurt you so that you can stand before God's throne with boldness as well as confidence; communicating with Him. You, believer in Jesus Christ, will participate in the wedding supper of the Lamb.

Revelation chapter 19 verse 9 says, "Then the angel said to me, "Write this: Blessed are those who are invited to the wedding supper of the Lamb!" And he added, "These are the true words of God." You just need to believe in Jesus' crucifixion and resurrection, your sins are forgiven by Jesus' blood that was shed, and to be waiting; expecting Jesus' return to participate in the wedding supper of the Lamb. As a glorified believer, the child of God, you will finally fulfill the purpose for which you have been created, which is complete, unbroken fellowship with God.

How do you define God's holy Church? God's holy Church is people believing in Jesus. It isn't a building that you go to weekly or a few times throughout the week. Nor is it a service you watch on T.V. or online. God's holy Church is professing or testifying believers who have faith in Jesus Christ, all throughout the world; from every tribe, every nation to every language. His holy Church is believers who know God and are spreading His gospel around. Spreading His gospel; making Jesus known is the one purpose that is the same for all believers in Jesus Christ. God's holy Church is unity and intimacy with God Himself. God will take care and nurture you as your loving Father. You feed and take care of your body that is how God will take care of you, His holy Church, but exceedingly and abundantly more! In Ephesians chapter 5 verses 29 through 30 say, "After all, no one ever hated their own body, but they feed and care for their body, just as Christ does the church—for we are members of his body."

It's easy to think when Jesus comes again on earth it will be a glorious day! There will be plagues on earth because God's wrath will be on people who don't apologize for their wrongs, evil desires, or turn to God to acknowledge that He is real! In Revelation chapter 6 verses 15 through 17 say, "Then the kings of the earth, the princes, the generals, the rich, the mighty, and everyone else, both slave and free, hid in caves and among the rocks of the mountains. They called to the mountains and the rocks, "Fall on us and hide us from the face of him who sits on the throne and from the wrath of the Lamb! For the great day of their wrath has come, and who can withstand it?"

Believers in Jesus Christ will also be resurrected from the dead just like Jesus was and is! You live in a body that can be called your earthly shell. Over time your body gets worn down and eventually, you pass away. God sent His Son, Jesus Christ onto the earth, away from His glory and majesty, and became a human being. Jesus grew up on the earth like you, but He never sinned. God's plan for Jesus was for Him to set the ultimate as well as the supreme example in living a holy and godly life that is pleasing to Him as an example for you! Also, Jesus had to be crucified on the cross so that you, as a believer, can have an intimate relationship with God and to be forgiven of your sins.

When Jesus along with His holy angels come to earth, people who have passed away will be resurrected from the dead. In the Gospel of Luke chapter 21 verses 25 through 27, Jesus says, "There will be signs in the sun, moon and stars. On the earth, nations will be in anguish and perplexity at the roaring and tossing of the sea. People will faint from terror, apprehensive of what is coming on the world, for the heavenly bodies will be shaken. At that time they will see the Son of Man coming in a cloud with power and great glory." The people who are resurrected from the dead will be witnesses and testify about Jesus to those who still don't believe in God.

It's your choice on where you want to spend eternity in. Do you want to be in Heaven with God, Jesus, Holy Spirit or in Hell, Hades being tormented in the Lake of Fire of burning sulfur? In 1st Thessalonians chapter 4 verses 13 through 18 the apostles Paul, Silas and Timothy say, "Brothers and sisters, we do not want you to be uninformed about those who sleep in death, so that you do not grieve like the rest of mankind, who have no hope. For we believe that Jesus died and rose again, and so we believe that God will bring with Jesus those who have fallen asleep in him. According to the Lord's word, we tell you that we who are still alive, who are left until the coming of the Lord, will certainly not precede those who have fallen asleep. For the Lord himself will come down from heaven, with a loud command, with the voice of the archangel and with the trumpet call of God, and the dead in Christ will rise first. After that, we who are still alive and are left will be caught up together with them in the clouds to meet the Lord in the air. And so we will be with the Lord forever. Therefore encourage one another with these words." Believers in Jesus Christ, who are still standing strong living by faith on the earth, will not go before other believers who have passed away and are in their graves. Believers in Jesus Christ will rise first, which refers to the resurrection of the dead, to be with the Lord forever.

Jesus' resurrection of the dead is essential because you, as believers can have intimate relationships with God and your sins are forgiven. You can have confidence in knowing that you will participate in the resurrection of the dead if you know that your name is written in the Lamb's Book of Life!

The resurrection of the dead refers to when believers in Jesus Christ are raised or caught up in the air to be with God forever. Your body or earthly suit changes into God's glory, full power, and to your spiritual body. The glorified body of Jesus Christ! In 1st Corinthians chapter 15 verses 51 through 57 Paul says, "Listen, I tell you a mystery: We will not all sleep, but we will all be changed—in a flash, in the twinkling of an eye, at the last trumpet. For the trumpet will sound, the dead will be raised imperishable, and we will be changed. For the perishable must clothe itself with the imperishable, and the mortal with immortality. When the perishable has been clothed with the imperishable, and the mortal with immortality, then the saying that is written will come true: "Death has been swallowed up in victory."

"Where, O death, is your victory? Where, O death, is your sting?" The sting of death is sin, and the power of sin is the law. But thanks be to God! He gives us the victory through our Lord Jesus Christ." What do imperishable, perishable, mortal, and immortality mean? Perishable is when you are dead and your body is decaying. Imperishable means that the glorified body of Jesus Christ will endure or last forever and ever. Mortal is you as a human being and so human beings will pass away because death is a part of life. It's just going to happen. Immortality means the ability to live forever, or eternal life. In 1st Corinthians chapter 15 verses 42 through 44 Paul says, "So will it be with the resurrection of the dead. The body that is sown is perishable, it is raised imperishable; it is sown in dishonor, it is raised in glory; it is sown in weakness, it is raised in power; it is sown a natural body, it is raised a spiritual body. If there is a natural body, there is also a spiritual body." Jesus had to experience the resurrection of the dead because He took away Satan's power of death and Hades (Hell,) and won the battle and brought victory for believers. Jesus got rid of death. If you believe, have faith in God, and are confident that your name is written in the Lamb's, Jesus' Book of Life, you will be a part of the resurrection of the dead; reigning with Christ for a thousand years! John says in Revelation chapter 21 verses 3 and 4, "And I heard a loud voice from the throne saying, "Look! God's dwelling place is now among the people, and he will dwell with them. They will be his people, and God himself will be with them and be their God. 'He will wipe every tear from their eyes. There will be no more death or mourning or crying or pain, for the old order of things has passed away."

God blessed you with the ability to make choices for choosing how you will live your life. Do you believe that God is 3

Persons in One? God is your Father. Jesus Christ is God's Son and the Holy Spirit is Jesus Himself dwelling within believers. Do you believe in the virgin birth? Personalize Jesus' crucifixion and resurrection by making His journey, was all for you because He loves you immensely; it's beyond understanding for God's love is unconditional! Jesus is seated at the right-hand of God, your Father and He will judge you based upon your heart and life. Your choices determine where you will spend eternity. It's either, Heaven with God, or in the Lake of Fire being tormented and separated from God, Jesus, Holy Spirit.

On to the next principle! Some of you think that baptism is when parents celebrate when their children are either infants or toddlers. Search and examine Scripture (the Bible) for yourself to see if what I am about to share is true. There four baptisms underneath the umbrella of instruction about cleansing rites of the nine principles in sound doctrine. You may become upset with me because I may stretch or go beyond your faith box, but it's alright. I will be persecuted for Jesus! Apostle Paul said in 1st Timothy chapter 4 verse 12, "Don't let anyone look down on you because you are young, but set an example for the believers in speech, in conduct, in love, in faith and in purity." The four baptisms are Baptism in water, Baptism in the Holy Spirit, Baptism of fire, and Baptism of the dead.

It's easy to think that everyone is going to Heaven because God is so loving and merciful that He won't send anyone to Hell. You could argue that whosoever believes in him shall not perish but have eternal life, in which Jesus says in the Gospel of John chapter 3 verse 16. God clearly says who will not inherit His kingdom in 1st Corinthians chapter 6 verses 9 and 10. These verses say, "Or do you not know that wrongdoers will not inherit the kingdom of God? Do not be deceived: Neither the sexually immoral nor idolaters nor adulterers nor men who have sex with men nor thieves nor the greedy nor drunkards nor slanderers nor swindlers will inherit the kingdom of God." When you aren't honoring God by loving, obeying, and serving Him wholeheartedly, you are living life how you want to, this means that you are living in the flesh. Living in the flesh is your lifestyle choices that don't please or honor God. Galatians chapter 5 verses 19 through 21 Paul says, "The acts of the flesh are obvious: sexual immorality, impurity and debauchery; idolatry and witchcraft; hatred, discord, jealousy, fits of rage, selfish ambition, dissensions, factions and envy; drunkenness, orgies, and the like. I warn you, as I did before, that those who live like this will not inherit the kingdom of God."

Baptism in water has different meanings. Some of you believe that it's a religious tradition. Babies are sprinkled on their foreheads or water is poured on their heads to be a part of God's family. A believer's baptism has a totally different meaning. For me, baptism meant to declare that I was finished following the authority of sin. I was deciding to obey God Almighty, Jesus Christ, and Holy Spirit in life. I was deciding to love, forgive, pray, and lend a helping hand in life. How I want to live is my choice. I can think that my desire is what satisfies. When I made the decision to surrender my life to Jesus Christ as my personal Lord and Savior and was baptized, I was set free from bondage. I have the incredible gift, blessing, and privilege from Lord God Almighty to believe, trust, and obey God my Father. In 2nd Corinthians chapter 5 verses 14 through 20, Paul explains how believers are restored lovingly and brought back to God after making the decision to make Jesus Christ their Lord and Savior. Paul says, "For Christ's love compels us, because we are convinced that one died for all, and therefore all died. And he died for all, that those who live should no longer live for themselves but for him who died for them and was raised again.

So from now on we regard no one from a worldly point of view. Though we once regarded Christ in this way, we do so no longer. Therefore, if anyone is in Christ, the new creation has come: The old has gone, the new is here! All this is from God, who reconciled us to himself through Christ and gave us the ministry of reconciliation: that God was reconciling the world to himself in Christ, not counting people's sins against them. And he has committed to us the message of reconciliation. We are therefore Christ's ambassadors, as though God were making his appeal through us."

Baptism in water is when you take the plunge and your body is submerged in water. You are saying that you are finished living a life that is consumed with sexual immorality, impurity and debauchery; idolatry and witchcraft; hatred, discord, jealousy, fits of rage, selfish ambition, drugs, alcohol, and partying; your body is under water. When your body is raised out of the water, this symbolizes that you are rising to live a new life following God's way. God will plant His seeds in the inside of you and He will care for you and help them grow as you partner with Him in living life honoring Him. The seeds are found in Galatians chapter 5 verses 22 and 23, which says, "But the fruit of the Spirit is love, joy, peace, forbearance, kindness, goodness, faithfulness, gentleness and self-control." You are created in God's image so God is transforming you into His fullness!

Jesus submerged His body in water because He was baptized, but when He came out of the water, He was baptized with the Holy Spirit. In the Gospel of Matthew chapter 3 verses 16 and 17 Matthew says, "As soon as Jesus was baptized, he went up out of the water. At that moment heaven was opened, and he saw the Spirit of God descending like a dove and alighting on him. And a voice from heaven said, "This is my Son, whom I love; with him I am well pleased."

The Scripture verses after this one explain how the Holy Spirit led Jesus into the wilderness to be tempted by Satan for 40 days and 40 nights. Satan doesn't want you to live life for God by putting God's command into action in life. Satan will do everything that he can do to tempt you into doing his evil schemes. You must submit to God, resist the devil, and he will flee from you as the Book of James chapter 4 verse 7 says to do.

Baptism in the Holy Spirit means God has brought you into His kingdom and the Holy Spirit is the power source in completing God's will on the earth. Literally, Jesus Himself is living and dwelling inside of you! Holy Spirit is God's still small voice enabling you to live a holy and godly life; being God's witnesses and testifying about Jesus through all the earth! In 2nd Timothy chapter 1 verse 7, Paul explains, "For God has not given to us the Spirit of fear, but of power, and of love, and of a sound mind." Holy Spirit helps you to be bold and confident when testifying about Jesus.

You must believe in your heart that Jesus Christ is Lord and by asking in prayer to God for His Holy Spirit to dwell within you, God will bless you with His Holy Spirit. Baptism in the Holy Spirit will enable you to speak in tongues. The gift of speaking in tongues is another way to pray to God; praying God's perfect will, and encouraging yourself. The Holy Spirit may enable you to prophesy, see visions, and dream dreams if you are baptized in Him. He will lead and guide you to do things for God. Holy Spirit will give you godly desires, such as reading God's Word, learning about God, having knowledge, and understanding of the Word of God. Also, Holy Spirit will give you the desire to lend a helping hand to others. Trust and obey Him because you are completing God's will. It won't make sense, but trust Him because God has a plan!

In 2nd Corinthians chapter 5 verse 20 Paul says, "We are therefore Christ's ambassadors, as though God were making his appeal through us." The definition of an ambassador is a person who represents or promotes something. So, you who believe in Jesus Christ, you are His spokesperson in the world; living and acting like Jesus, showing the world that Jesus is real. You must be urgent in living life as Jesus lived on the earth. Jesus' life is described in the four gospels of God's Word. Many of you think that life as well as time lasts forever. Life is short and everything will change in the blink of an eye. It's a vapor, such as a mist of perfume or cologne, you spray it; for a moment you can smell the scent, then in the next moment you don't smell it. Life is like that; it's here today, but tomorrow it won't be because tomorrow isn't a guarantee.

Jesus taught His disciples how to pray to God and the prayer is a model or an outline for all believers. The prayer is in the Gospel of Matthew chapter 6 verses 9 through 15, which says, "This, then, is how you should pray: "'Our Father in heaven, hallowed be your name, your kingdom come, your will be done, on earth as it is in heaven. Give us today our daily bread. And forgive us our debts, as we also have forgiven our debtors. And lead us not into temptation, but deliver us from the evil one. For if you forgive other people when they sin against you, your heavenly Father will also forgive you. But if you do not forgive others their sins, your Father will not forgive your sins." The phrases "your kingdom come, your will be done, on earth as it is in heaven" have a heavier meaning. God's kingdom is the Holy Spirit living inside of you if you ask God for His Holy Spirit. God blesses you with His Holy Spirit and you have the power plus the authority to do God's will here on earth as it is in Heaven. If you believe and have faith in Jesus Christ, you can command evil spirits or sicknesses and diseases to be bound or to leave and they will flee because there aren't evil spirits, sicknesses or diseases in Heaven. You can pray for God to send His angels to keep watch over you because God loosens and blesses you with good gifts. God's kingdom is in the inside of you. You just need to know how to use the power and the authority. By faith in Jesus Christ, Jesus' Name is powerful. He gives you His power and authority to share His gospel with others, comfort those who are hurting, and to free those who Satan has bound in darkness and slavery, and to help them see that only Jesus can completely satisfy them!

The baptism in the Holy Spirit is when believers place their hands on you when you desire to be Spirit-filled; Holy Spirit dwelling on the inside of you. You must believe that you have received the baptism in the Holy Spirit. In the Book of Acts chapter 8 verses 14 through 17 the apostles explain how believers received the Holy Spirit. "When the apostles in Jerusalem heard that Samaria had accepted the word of God, they sent Peter and John to Samaria. When they arrived, they prayed for the new believers there that they might receive the Holy Spirit, because the Holy Spirit had not yet come on any of them; they had simply been baptized in the name of the Lord Jesus. Then Peter and John placed their hands on them, and they received the Holy Spirit." The laying on of hands belief means one of two things. First, it can mean that you are asking God for a blessing for other people. Second, you have the authority by having faith in Jesus to pray for strength, power, healing, and protection for others. The laying on of hands is a principle of sound doctrine that I explain later.

When you are Spirit-filled you may not understand or be able to explain your knowledge as well as wisdom that you share because of your faith. Living life in the Spirit and in God's truths mean that there will be times that you don't or won't completely understand what Holy Spirit is telling you to do or why He is telling you to say something. In the Gospel of John, Jesus explains this. John chapter 3 verse 8 Jesus says, "The wind blows wherever it pleases. You hear its sound, but you cannot tell where it comes from or where it is going. So it is with everyone born of the Spirit." There will be times in your relationship with God that the Holy Spirit will say, "No" to you to avoid danger. Being baptized in the Holy Spirit, you are blessed with this awareness or inner peace. That's Jesus leading and guiding you in life! Sometimes He won't give you His peace for a certain situation to lead and guide you from a bad circumstance. But He will always be with you through it.

Holy Spirit is the Helper, in which He teaches you the awesome and incredible mysteries of God! He won't do everything for you. Think of Him as your coach and teammate; you must complete your part and vice versa, in which Holy Spirit will do His part in your relationship. He gives you boldness and the confidence in speaking God's Word and testifying about Jesus to others. In the Book of Acts chapter 4 verse 31 the apostles say, "After they prayed, the place where they were meeting was shaken. And they were all filled with the Holy Spirit and spoke the word of God boldly."

Remember you are Jesus' example in the world; God's kingdom and Jesus Himself is in you if you believe in Him and obey His commands. God blesses you with His power and authority to ask for healing in Jesus' Name, to give strength or encouragement to others, and to testify about Him. Baptism in the Holy Spirit is completing God's will on the earth. Being Spirit-filled and Spirit-led won't make sense, but God's plan is coming into completion!

God has a specific purpose and plan for your life. It's easy to think about all of the negatives and the reasons why God can't use you. The reasons can be: you don't speak well, you're too old or you're too young, you're overweight, you're not educated enough, your family is broken, or you are disabled. The sound doctrine principle of baptism of fire is when God speaks to you or gives you a desire to do something for His glory. The desires can be things, such as being a doctor, nurse, lawyer, police officer, fire fighter, and joining the army or the navy. Also, the desires can be being married, raising children, being a teacher, serving others, or being an author. Baptism of fire is when God is preparing you to do His will, plan, and mission. In the Book of Exodus chapter 3, an angel of the Lord appeared to Moses in the form of a burning bush. God's people, the Israelites had been forced into slavery by Pharaoh and the Egyptians. Exodus chapter 3 verses 7 through 10 say, "The LORD said, "I have indeed seen the misery of my people in Egypt. I have heard them crying out because of their slave drivers, and I am concerned about their suffering. So I have come down to rescue them from the hand of the Egyptians and to bring them up out of that land into a good and spacious land, a land flowing with milk and honey—the home of the Canaanites, Hittites, Amorites, Perizzites, Hivites and Jebusites. And now the cry of the Israelites has reached me, and I have seen the way the Egyptians are oppressing them. So now, go. I am sending you to Pharaoh to bring my people the Israelites out of Egypt."

This seemed like a good plan, didn't it? Moses took the Israelites out under Pharaoh's control, out of slavery, and into a good and spacious land, a land flowing with milk and honey. Wait just a moment! Pharaoh didn't free the Israelites easily. He fought against God, Moses, and Aaron. Aaron was Moses' brother who helped Moses speak to the people, Pharaoh, and performed the signs and wonders that God blessed Moses and Aaron with the abilities to do them. The signs and wonders were: Moses' staff turned into a snake, Moses' hand turned leprous when Moses reached his hand in his cloak and when Moses put his hand back into his cloak his hand was restored back to normal. Other signs were the Nile River turned into blood, frogs, gnats, flies covered the earth, the Egyptians' livestock died, boils, hail and locusts' plagues, the plagues of darkness and every firstborn of the Egyptians dead.

All these signs and wonders that God blessed Moses and Aaron to perform brought opposition or resistance from people and things. This is how it will be in your life to block you from completing God's mission. In this story of when Moses took the Israelites out of the land of slavery, Pharaoh's heart was hardened and he wouldn't let the Israelites go into a good and spacious land to worship God. During this process God was molding and maturing everyone's heart for the journey ahead.

When I was eight years old, God put the desire in my heart to be a published author. I wanted to write books in hopes of people seeing that I was smart to help them look pass my disability. Through the years of my life, I have experienced triumphs and tragedies like you have gone through to mature me into God's daughter whom He intended me to be and for His purpose! It took 18 years for God's plan of being a published author to come into existence.

The baptism of fire may take time to harvest or come into existence. God puts good desires in hearts for His glory and purpose! Think about how plants grow. They start out as a seed. Over a large amount of time plants grow to become their full potential. God has a purpose for your life and you were born for such a time as this! In 1st Corinthians chapter 10 verse 31 Paul says, "So whether you eat or drink or whatever you do, do it all for the glory of God." Jesus will judge you on how you lived on earth so if your heart is right before Jesus, you will enter Heaven. If you have good deeds that you completed in your lifetime, Jesus will test them in fire, which is referring to the baptism of fire, to see if your good deeds will survive, you will then receive a reward. If your good deeds are burned up, you will suffer loss but yet will be saved—even though only as one escaping through the flames. All you need to be saved is believe in Jesus like the thief on the cross did when Jesus was crucified! The thief didn't have to do good deeds. He was being crucified. Although faith produces or at least should produce good deeds in your life, but all that matters is faith coming from a pure heart!

The last of the four baptisms underneath the umbrella of instruction about cleansing rites of the nine principles in sound doctrine is the baptism of the dead. Someone may argue that you need to be baptized for the dead. Yet you may not believe in the resurrection of the dead. You are contradicting the truth. 1st Corinthians chapter 15 verse 29 Paul asks, "Now if there is no resurrection, what will those do who are baptized for the dead? If the dead are not raised at all, why are people baptized for them?"

In the letter to the Romans chapter 12 verse 2 Paul urges all believers in Jesus Christ to think for themselves and to not follow the world or its' direction. Paul says, "Do not conform to the pattern of this world, but be transformed by the renewing of your mind. Then you will be able to test and approve what God's will is—his good, pleasing and perfect will." God blessed you with a brain so complete research for yourself to see and stand firm on your beliefs. Quit being lazy so that you can have a thorough conversation with someone if he or she believes that there is a baptism of the dead practice.

The seventh principle of sound doctrine is the laying on of hands and this means that you are asking God for a blessing. You believe that God will do what He wants according to His Word because of your devotion to God is firm and unshakable. The belief of laying on of hands means that you have the authority by having faith in Jesus to pray for strength, power, healing, and protection for others. God is the One who gives the blessing. When a believer of Jesus Christ desires the gift of the Holy Spirit and the gifts of the Spirit, fellow believers will place their hands on the believer and God will bless him or her with His Holy Spirit and other gifts as He determines.

God's Word, Bible is split in two parts; the first is called Old Testament and the other is called New Testament. People who lived in the Old Testament, lived under the Ten Commandments which is consider to be the law before Jesus Christ was crucified on the cross, in which He made a new covenant established on better promises. During the Old Testament times, people's hands or exchanging of attire like sandals were what they used for making something legal because they didn't have contracts to sign. Receiving a blessing by the laying on of hands is comparable with receiving your inheritance so it was a big deal. In the Book of Genesis, Joseph's father, Jacob or Israel blesses Joseph's sons by laying his hands on them. Genesis chapter 48 verses 13 through 16 say, "And Joseph took both of them, Ephraim on his right toward Israel's left hand and Manasseh on his left toward Israel's right hand, and brought them close to him. But Israel reached out his right hand and put it on Ephraim's head, though he was the younger, and crossing his arms, he put his left hand on Manasseh's head, even though Manasseh was the firstborn. Then he blessed Joseph and said, "May the God before whom my fathers Abraham and Isaac walked faithfully, the God who has been my shepherd all my life to this day, the Angel who has delivered me from all harm —may he bless these boys. May they be called by my name and the names of my fathers Abraham and Isaac, and may they increase greatly on the earth." The continuation of this story shows how Joseph was displeased with his father because his father made the older son serve the younger son and by making the younger son be greater. Genesis chapter 49 is the blessings that Jacob or Israel gave to his sons before he died.

In the Gospel of Luke, there are many instances, in which people were healed when someone laid his or her hands on them. Jesus raised a widow's son back to life. Luke chapter 7 verses 14 through 15 say, "Then he went up and touched the bier they were carrying him on, and the bearers stood still. He said, "Young man, I say to you, get up!" The dead man sat up and began to talk, and Jesus gave him back to his mother."" A bier is when a dead body is being carried for burial.

Jesus placed His hands on a crippled woman and healed her. Luke chapter 13 verses 10 through 13 say, "On a Sabbath Jesus was teaching in one of the synagogues, and a woman was there who had been crippled by a spirit for eighteen years. She was bent over and could not straighten up at all. When Jesus saw her, he called her forward and said to her, "Woman, you are set free from your infirmity." Then he put his hands on her, and immediately she straightened up and praised God."

Jesus placed His hands on children to bless them. God is a forgiving and compassionate God. In the Gospel of Mark, Mark says in chapter 10 verses 13 through 16, "People were bringing little children to Jesus for him to place his hands on them, but the disciples rebuked them. When Jesus saw this, he was indignant. He said to them, "Let the little children come to me, and do not hinder them, for the kingdom of God belongs to such as these. Truly I tell you, anyone who will not receive the kingdom of God like a little child will never enter it." And he took the children in his arms, placed his hands on them and blessed them."

By faith in Jesus and the desire to be healed, you will be healed. In Acts of the Apostles, Acts chapter 3 verses 2 through 10 say, "Now a man who was lame from birth was being carried to the temple gate called Beautiful, where he was put every day to beg from those going into the temple courts. When he saw Peter and John about to enter, he asked them for money. Peter looked straight at him, as did John. Then Peter said, "Look at us!" So the man gave them his attention, expecting to get something from them. Then Peter said, "Silver or gold I do not have, but what I do have I give you. In the name of Jesus Christ of Nazareth, walk." Taking him by the right hand, he helped him up, and instantly the man's feet and ankles became strong. He jumped to his feet and began to walk. Then he went with them into the temple courts, walking and jumping, and praising God. When all the people saw him walking and praising God, they recognized him as the same man who used to sit begging at the temple gate called Beautiful, and they were filled with wonder and amazement at what had happened to him." I have had many believers who assumed that I wanted to be healed from my disability and quoted Scripture verses of Jesus healing people. I have had people who prayed over me because I was not confident enough to say, "No, thank you." I had even gone to the extent of having believers assist me out of my wheelchair and helped me take steps in a big circle because I didn't speak up to say, "No." Sure I face daily challenges more than you and that does not bother me because my aim is on seeking God, knowing Him, and helping others know Him intimately. I do not understand the reasons behind life's circumstances unfolding. I can step out in faith to know that God will do what He wants. Time is becoming shorter until the day that Jesus comes back on the earth. As a child of God, I need to be spreading the gospel. Others may not stand up for Jesus. God created me unique! I have a purpose that God made for me and only I can fulfill it.

Believers in Jesus Christ, you can lay your hands on fellow believers to send them out into the mission field to preach, teach, and share God's Word to others. The mission field doesn't necessarily mean a third world country. It means where you are and the community that you surround yourself with. In God's Word some people showed others to the apostles so that they laid their hands on the people. These people were known for their faith and obedience to the Holy Spirit so they were considered to be sent out to spread God's Word. Acts chapter 6 verse 6 says, "They presented these men to the apostles, who prayed and laid their hands on them."

Holy Spirit leads, guides, and provides you into God's ways. He is your Helper because He will teach and remind you of what God says in His Word depending on your faith and obedience to Him. Also, He will warn you so that you can avoid terrible things. If you believe and have faith in God, God blesses you with His Holy Spirit. You can be a believer of Jesus Christ and not have the Holy Spirit dwelling within you. This is what happened to the apostles. Acts chapter 8 verses 14 through 17 say, "When the apostles in Jerusalem heard that Samaria had accepted the word of

God, they sent Peter and John to Samaria. When they arrived, they prayed for the new believers there that they might receive the Holy Spirit, because the Holy Spirit had not yet come on any of them; they had simply been baptized in the name of the Lord Jesus. Then Peter and John placed their hands on them, and they received the Holy Spirit."

Jesus blesses you, His child with the gift of placing your hands on sick people and they will get well (Mark chapter 16 verse 18). But you must believe in Jesus with your whole being; not swaying in unbelief, but having confidence in knowing Jesus will do what is in accordance with His Word and will. God can use you for healing people depending on your faith and obedience to Him. Yet God is the One who gives the healing. Paul was transformed into a spokesman for the gospel of Jesus Christ and in Acts chapter 28 verses 7 through 9 displays how God used Paul because he trusted God to heal a sick person by the belief and the sound doctrine principle of the laying on of hands, "There was an estate nearby that belonged to Publius, the chief official of the island. He welcomed us to his home and showed us generous hospitality for three days. His father was sick in bed, suffering from fever and dysentery. Paul went in to see him and, after prayer, placed his hands on him and healed him. When this had happened, the rest of the sick on the island came and were cured."

1st Timothy chapter 5 verse 22 says, "Do not be hasty in the laying on of hands, and do not share in the sins of others. Keep yourself pure." Don't be in a hurry to bless someone who you don't know how he or she lives life. Have patience and this certain someone will prove him or herself to the Church. The gifts that God has blessed the person with will demonstrate for themselves. Yet this person's goal shouldn't be to have the pastors or the elders of the church lay their hands on him or her to receive a title in the church. Then this person is concerned about his or her image rather than serving God. You and I have our own sins so we don't need to partake in others' sins.

Believing in Jesus Christ and passionately living out His gospel, God will bless you with the gift of the laying on of hands. By God's power and authority, you can give the blessing in prayer for strength, power, healing, and protection for others by the laying on of hands. Just remember don't rush to lay hands on others when you don't know their motive. God blesses you with His Holy Spirit to help you by leading, guiding, and providing for you to live a godly life; not lacking in any spiritual gift. The laying on of hands blesses you to do God's will for His ministry. In obedience to Jesus Christ, in humility, yet in boldness and confidence lay hands on others to spread faith around in this dark world!

Now I will explain Jesus resurrection from the dead (the eighth principle of sound doctrine) and how you as a believer will also be resurrected. Lazarus, the brother of Mary and Martha, was resurrected from the dead. Lazarus was a friend of Jesus who had passed away and his body laid in a grave or a cave for four days. Some of the people were insulting Jesus by saying that He opened the eyes of the blind and yet He couldn't save Lazarus from dying. Jesus prayed to God because of the people's unbelief of Him. In the Gospel of John chapter 11 verses 41 through 44 say, "So they took away the stone. Then Jesus looked up and said, "Father, I thank you that you have heard me. I knew that you always hear me, but I said this for the benefit of the people standing here, that they may believe that you sent me." When he had said this, Jesus called in a loud voice, "Lazarus, come out!" The dead man came out, his hands and feet wrapped with strips of linen, and a cloth around his face. Jesus said to them, "Take off the grave clothes and let him go." Lazarus was resurrected from the dead and in the Gospel of John chapter 12 verse 2 John mentions Lazarus reclined at the table in Jesus' presence while the Passover meal was taking place.

God sent His Son, Jesus Christ onto the earth, away from His glory and majesty, and became a human being like you. Jesus grew up on the earth, but He never sinned. God's plan for Jesus was for Him to set the ultimate as well as the supreme example in living a holy and godly life that is pleasing to God! Also, Jesus had to be crucified on the cross so that you, as believer, can have an intimate relationship with God and to be forgiven of your sins.

Jesus was defeating Satan and death when Jesus' body was laid in the tomb for two days. On the third day, Jesus was raised to life! Jesus paid the ultimate price to save and release you from death by being crucified. Jesus saved you from death and Satan's authority in your life. Satan's goal is to separate you from God, but Jesus defeated him and took away his power. For nothing, in all creation will be able to separate you from the love of God that is in Christ Jesus your Lord.

A believer who is standing strong living by faith on the earth, will not go before other believers who have passed away and are in their graves. Believers in Jesus Christ will rise first, which refers to the resurrection of the dead, to be with the Lord forever. In 1st Thessalonians chapter 4 verses 13 through 18 the apostles Paul, Silas and Timothy say, "Brothers and sisters, we do not want you to be uninformed about those who sleep in death, so that you do not grieve like the rest of mankind, who have no hope. For we believe that Jesus died and rose again, and so we believe that God will bring with Jesus those who have fallen asleep in him. According to the Lord's word, we tell you that we who are still alive, who are left until the coming of the Lord, will certainly not precede those who have fallen asleep. For the Lord himself will come down from heaven, with a loud command, with the voice of the archangel and with the trumpet call of God, and the dead in Christ will rise first. After that, we who are still alive and are left will be caught up together with them in the clouds to meet the Lord in the air. And so we will be with the Lord forever. Therefore encourage one another with these words."

Now it's time to explain the last principle of sound doctrine which is eternal judgment. Jesus Christ is your Judge and will judge your actions in how you lived your life on the earth. The secrets of all hearts will be brought to light because Jesus will judge you. Did you live your life that pleased and honored God; following His commands with all your heart, desired to follow God in every season of life? Or did you live life doing what you wanted to do whenever you wanted to do it? You lived life carefree.

You will stand before the judgment seat of God, in which your whole life books will be opened as well as the Lamb's Book of Life! Your life books contain every good and bad action as well as thought that you have done. If you lived life honoring God and you remained faithful to Him until the very end, Jesus will reward you for your continued faithfulness to Him. But if you lived life the opposite of what pleased and honored God, you will suffer loss. If your good deeds are burned up, you will suffer loss but yet will be saved—even though only as one escaping through the flames (1st Corinthians chapter 3 verse 15). All you need to be saved is believe in Jesus like the thief on the cross did when Jesus was crucified! Believe in your heart, confess with your lips that Jesus is Lord and you shall be saved!

In life there are 2 types of deaths that you will experience which they are called First Death and Second Death. The First Death refers to when your body is dead and you aren't a human being any longer. It's the separation of body and soul. The Second Death is the disapproval of souls for their destination to eternal punishment. It's the final penalty of the unrighteous. Unrighteous means you are not upright or virtuous; you are wicked; sinful, and evil. Your behavior and character were not honorable or honest while you lived on the earth. You did not believe that Jesus died to pay for your sins. With God, there is no favoritism. Romans chapter 3 verse 23 Paul says, "for all have sinned and fall short of the glory of God." God knows what is in your heart and loves you more than you could possibly understand in your body. Human beings have limited understanding of things just because of human nature. Human nature is the ways that you think, feel, and act naturally.

You will be tormented day and night in the Lake of Fire of burning sulfur if you did not ask for salvation in Jesus Christ. In the book of Revelation chapter 20 verses 12 through 15 John says, "And I saw the dead, small and great, stand before God; and the books were opened: and another book was opened, which is the book of life: and the dead were judged out of those things which were written in the books, according to their works. And the sea gave up the dead which were in it; and death and hell delivered up the dead which were in them: and they were judged every man according to their works. And death and hell were cast into the lake of fire. This is the second death. And whosoever was not found written in the book of life was cast into the lake of fire."

If you lived victoriously on earth, believed in Jesus with all your heart, soul, and mind; honored God in everything, faced persecutions and hardships because of your faith in Jesus Christ; stood firm and endured until the end, your name is written in the Lamb's Book of Life! You will receive your reward, such as a mansion in Heaven according to your good deeds deserve. Jesus says in the Gospel of John chapter 14 verses 2 through 3, "My Father's house has many rooms; if that were not so, would I have told you that I am going there to prepare a place for you? And if I go and prepare a place for you, I will come back and take you to be with me that you also may be where I am."

When the time comes in accordance to God's perfect timing, there will be a New Heaven and a New Earth for this old earth as well as the present evil age will pass away. God will make everything new; the way God intended humanity to be since the creation of the world! In Revelation chapter 21 verses 3 through 5 a loud voice from the throne says, "Look! God's dwelling place is now among the people, and he will dwell with them. They will be his people, and God himself will be with them and be their God. 'He will wipe every tear from their eyes. There will be no more death or mourning or crying or pain, for the old order of things has passed away." He who was seated on the throne said, "I am making everything new!"

In Revelation chapter 21 verses 7 through 8 Jesus says, "Those who are victorious will inherit all this, and I will be their God and they will be my children. But the cowardly, the unbelieving, the vile, the murderers, the sexually immoral, those who practice magic arts, the idolaters and all liars—they will be consigned to the fiery lake of burning sulfur. This is the second death." God is a gentle, merciful, and loving Father. He won't force you to be in an intimate relationship with Him if you don't want to. God blesses you with free choice; freedom to choose how to live your life. Your choices determine where you will spend eternity. It's either, Heaven with God, or in the Lake of Fire being tormented and separated from God, Jesus, Holy Spirit forever!

In 2nd Timothy chapter 4 verse 3 Paul says, "For the time will come when people will not put up with sound doctrine. Instead, to suit their own desires, they will gather around them a great number of teachers to say what their itching ears want to hear." Many of you know me while there are others who don't know me. You might know that I have the physical disability of Cerebral Palsy and my speech can be difficult to understand. You may feel appalled after reading this book. You may be thinking that I don't have the authority to write this. It's alright. I understand the reasons behind your thoughts because I have had these thoughts. In 1st Timothy chapter 4 verse 12 Paul says, "Don't let anyone look down on you because you are young, but set an example for the believers in speech, in conduct, in love, in faith and in purity." With the help of the Holy Spirit, my aim was to help you thoroughly understand the nine principles that are fundamental to believers in Jesus Christ. Now that you read this, I hope you are able to have conversations with others regarding salvation in Jesus Christ so that they can declare that Jesus is their Lord and Savior. But not just that, I hope that you will be able to explain the repentance from acts that lead to death, faith in God, the four baptisms, the laying on of hands, the resurrection of the dead, and the eternal judgment sound doctrine principles to others. Spread God's gospel into the world by being Jesus' hands and feet.

About The Author

Emily surrounded her life as well as declared Jesus Christ as being her Lord and Savior in October of 2009. During 2020, God blessed her with the time to study and write about the nine sound doctrine principles.

Emily believes that the Bible is the Word of God and God, Jesus Christ, Holy Spirit speaks to believers through Scripture. Emily has humbled herself and desires to understand who God is personally. God helped Emily to understand that He wrote all Scripture; the Word of God is useful for teaching, rebuking, correcting, and training to have a clear conscience before Him so that she can be transformed into His glorious image.

Emily has published Open H†S Word, Chap†er By Chap†er, Dimly Lit, and Spiri† Wri††en Life as well with God's help.

www.ingramcontent.com/pod-product-compliance
Lightning Source LLC
Chambersburg PA
CBHW070947120626
46546CB00004B/1609